Colle_

The Ultimate Student's Guide for Choosing the Best College Major For You

within is the solitary and utter responsibility of the recipient reader. Under no circumstances will any legal responsibility or blame be held against the publisher for any reparation, damages, or monetary loss due to the information herein, either directly or indirectly.

The information herein is offered for informational purposes solely, and is universal as so. The presentation of the information is without contract or any type of guarantee assurance.

The trademarks that are used are without any consent, and the publication of the trademark is without permission or backing by the trademark owner. All trademarks and brands within this book are for clarifying purposes only and are the owned by the owners themselves, not affiliated with this document.

Table Of Contents

Introduction

This short book contains proven steps and strategies on how to select the college major that best suits your needs. If you are a recent high school graduate or a college student who's undecided on your major, this book can potentially be a great resource for you.

Choosing a college major can be one of the biggest decisions a person makes in their young adult life. There is pressure coming from all different directions, including parents, siblings, friends, and even classmates. It's important that you have as much critical information as you can get possibly your hands on, in order to make the best decision for your future.

This book will serve useful if you make sure to implement what you learn in the following pages. The important thing is that you

IMPLEMENT what you learn. Choosing a college major isn't a simple 30 minute pondering process, but the important thing to remember is that if you put in the necessary research and effort up front, you will be saving money, time, and disappointment in the long run.

Many people enter college with no clear path of what they want to accomplish and before they know it, they've wasted thousands of dollars without feeling any sense of fulfillment. Needless to say, with so many majors to choose from, it can be overwhelming to narrow down which one is the best for you. This book will serve as your pathfinder towards a college major that best suits your strengths and capabilities. So don't panic or stress yourself out!

It is recommended that you take notes while you are reading this book. This will ensure that you get the most out of the information in here. The notes will help you to pinpoint exactly what you need to focus on and by writing things down, you will be able to recall specifics on how to handle the tough decisions that you will face.

Lastly, it is encouraged that you do your own research on the topics that you want to look deeper into. To choose the correct college major, it will take some work on your part but you can do it! So remember to read with confidence and an open mind!

Chapter 1:

Reflect on Passion

Before you make any big decision, you should begin by finding out about yourself, being clear about your interests, and knowing your abilities as well as your values. What activities do you enjoy engaging in? What do you want from your academic major? Most importantly, what are your strengths and weaknesses that you can offer to the marketplace?

Pursuing a career after college is a common thing. Pursuing a career that one really loves is another story. In reality, one of the reasons why people do not succeed with their careers is that they are not pleased with what they do. Many people are not content with their jobs, simply because it wasn't actually their field of interest. After a decade or so of being dissatisfied with work, many people feel that it is either too late for them to make the change to a more fulfilling career path, or they do not want to risk giving up what they have built.

Avoid putting yourself in a similar situation by discovering what your most ideal career path is. Think of your interests and write them in a diary or journal. You will probably have a lot of them if you are a curious individual, but you need to trim them down through a quick and easy activity as you move on with this exercise.

Also, include the things you are truly curious about. Why? These curiosities are stored deep in your consciousness and you often neglect their potential to lead you to success. A visual cue (text or picture) of these things compels you to act on the more immediate and more realistic ones. Without noticing it, you are already changing them into interests and then into things you are passionate about.

A perfect example of an astoundingly successful worldwide figure with an interesting case of curiosity was Steve Jobs. He was extremely curious regarding how typefaces worked, so much so that he enrolled in a typography class when he was attending college. During his time, studying typography would have been considered a waste of time and money because it wasn't directly correlated with his degree plan.

However, Steve thought otherwise. What he learned from the subject developed his design sensibilities, and the rest is history. He used this sensibility to help the company he co-founded, Apple Incorporated, to thrive within the dynamic and uber-competitive field of technology. Today, a lot of innovations, not only by Apple, but also in the world of digital technology, are credited to Steve Jobs and his method of thinking.

While making a list of your interests, you will definitely find yourself dealing with many of them. Quantity is not what you are after though, especially with the task at hand, which is to determine the most valuable among hundreds of college majors possibly offered by thousands of colleges and universities within the country, or even abroad. Reduce your burden by qualifying these interests with the question, "which among these would you pursue if you had a million dollars?"

Assign a minimum of a hundred thousand dollars on each interest you strongly believe you could excel at. Depending on your gut feel, raise the value of some items until you exhaust the imaginary million dollars. Halfway through the activity, you should have a maximum of ten interests or a minimum of one. At face value, you might think it is the interest with the highest dollar amount that you would want to pursue and base your college major from, but not quite - until you move on to the last part of the activity.

Back to your list, remove all assigned dollar values and ask yourself, "which of these would I still pursue now that I've lost all my money?"

So, what's the point?

As soon as you find yourself compelled to limit your interests to the best of the best, you are already preparing yourself for college. Choosing a college major requires a balance between your financial capability and your passion. In a more realistic world though, passion always outweighs money. This is why you still find yourself choosing what you want to do in spite of losing that imaginary million dollars.

As you probably already know, with the amount of money it takes to pay for a college degree these days, nobody wants to end up pursuing the wrong college major, and in due course, the wrong career.

Knowing your passion is the most basic thing to consider in choosing a college major. You need to know yourself first. The issue is that most people know what they want but they still end up not following their passion for a number of reasons. We can't blame them, for they have their own reasons and there are several factors that affect decision making. Parents and friends can often times negatively affect the decision a young person makes on their future and that is very unfortunate.

It is sometimes difficult not to be influenced by the people around you, especially by your parents. However, there is a way for you to re-direct these positive influences back to them while reinforcing what you want to do with your future.

If you're like most young adults, your parents will most likely encourage you to pursue a college degree similar to theirs, or anything that will lead you to the same career path or financial stability they walked on. Of course this is well and good if you are strongly inclined to follow their lead, but what about when their plans do not fit with yours?

Many times, young people fail to acknowledge what good plans their parents have for them. They easily feel misunderstood and neglected, but few wonder why their parents had to make the plans for them. The answer is that, often times, no one ever showed them that they too could develop a plan of their own.

As soon as you possibly can, communicate your intentions to your parents. If you get caught in between disagreements, try relating the many positive traits you acquired from them to an interest you want to pursue as a career. Are they willfully strong? Are either of them as inquisitive as you are? Use their positive traits to mirror your career plans. Doing so can help you get their agreement on your college major proposal.

Most importantly, let them witness your dedication. Engage in activities that further your interests. Accomplish as many goals and successes from those activities. For example, join an amateur photography club and as many photo competitions to reinforce your plans of pursuing a career in this field. Once they see that you are excelling in your area of interest, they are most likely to leave you in deciding which college major to pursue.

As for your friends, do not let their opinions get in the way of following your passion. At the end of the day, your priority is your own happiness. Even though many young adults know their friends are not very wise and their judgment shouldn't be valued too highly, the feeling of peer pressure can still become overwhelming.

Regardless, if your friends are true, you should not have any issue getting their support in pursuing an interest, a college major, or a career that you love. If anything, use your closest friends as consultants regarding your interests and personality. Often times, they know your tendencies and quirks better than your family members.

You are as aware as anyone of your inner strengths and capabilities. It can't be stressed enough how important it is to evaluate your strengths, weaknesses, and interests based on your own inner guidance. Looking to others to tell you what major to choose is a very dangerous path that many young people go down and regret it later on down the line. You are the person that is going to live with the results of your decisions before it affects anyone else.

If you struggle to pinpoint these characteristics in yourself, a great place to start is by asking your closest friends, family members, and teachers what you seem to be passionate about in conversation and what your strong personality traits are. After taking this information into account, make sure to write it down and see if you can come to your own conclusions from there. You may realize things about yourself that you never thought about before.

Be as brutally honest about your shortcomings and dislikes as possible. For example, if you know you are a high energy and active person, working a desk job for ten hours per day is not for you. Don't ignore these obvious character traits or preferences and attempt to convince yourself that you can override them somehow. Focus on as much alignment as possible.

Another important point to consider regarding financials - according to Stephanie Balmer, Admissions Dean at Dickinson College, it's best to take classes in which you're going to be confident in. If you choose one that's among the highest paying college majors, you will be guaranteed to be happy, right? Think again!

When it comes to the highest earning college majors, young people do not usually look past the glamour. For example, are you the type of person that wants to spend 15-18 hours a day working on an oil reserve in the Gulf of Mexico? Well, if you didn't look further, you'd think Petroleum Engineering is the best college degree to get because it pays over $85,000 at many entry level positions right out of college.

Money will always be an important factor in our lives as a developed society. However, money matters, but only to a certain extent. Happiness later on in your life won't be based on your income as much as how much you enjoy the day-to-day process of what you are doing. They say money can't buy happiness but without a comfortable lifestyle it is definitely harder to be happy because of all the undue stresses. Financial compensation is an important factor, but only until you can provide a comfortable lifestyle for yourself and your family!

We will go deeper into the financial side later on, but for now, remember that for most people college is maybe 4-7 years total. After that, you are going to be spending decades working! Is that high salary going to be enough to keep you happy when you are 45 years old going into work at 7am and staying late to finish that tough project you have no excitement for?

Michelle Perry Higgins, a financial planner and principal at California Financial Advisors, advises students to major in a subject that really motivates them, more than placing their future salary considerations first. She advises to do what you love every day, work hard, and be honest. She believes in choosing a major where one is passionate about the work and can see themselves maintaining that passion despite market forces.

As noted by Dr. Randall S. Hansen, founder of www.quintcareers.com Quintessential Careers — one of the oldest and most comprehensive career development sites on the Web, the majority of students arrive on campus and do not know exactly what their major and career ambitions are going to be.

Steve Jobs' speech to Stanford graduates can inspire you to follow where your heart is. As quoted, you have to trust in something — your gut, destiny, life, karma. In the end, it will help to listen to your soul. Once you go after what you love, even if it does not make as much money, it will be worth your time in the long run.

If you are having trouble pinpointing your passions, and the feedback from the people in your life isn't enough, you can partake in a few different exercises that will help to guide you:

Try keeping track of all the things you search out for during the day. Look at your internet search queries, the books or posters in your room, the conversations you are having with different people, and most importantly, the thoughts that you think about when you are alone.

By keeping track of all these patterns of thought and interaction, you will begin to see patterns of what you spend a lot of your waking time concerned about. It may seem silly at first, but deep introspection is the best way to find these true passions. In today's world, most high school and college students are so distracted by social media and their phones, that they do not even designate any time to think about what makes them unique, inspired, and alive.

Chapter 2:

How Much Will It Cost?

It's time for a reality check. Now that you already have an idea of what your passion(s) are, the next thing we need to figure out is how much it is going to cost you if you decide to pursue a college degree. Many, though not all, people who are unemployed with a college degree made the mistake of not choosing a college major that is in demand, and provides salaries that are high enough to justify the cost of their tuition.

The truth is that many majors that are offered at large universities may be extremely interesting or even intuitively seem like they would provide well-paying jobs at an entry-level position. The problem is that, without research, we won't be able to predict which majors will be in demand and which may become overly susceptible to the economic climate, automated, or even completely gone in the future.

Historically, the most well-paying majors you can choose from are the "STEM" majors. STEM stands for Science, Technology, Engineering & Mathematics. These majors look to be, and have been, in high demand for a very long time because the world is always in need of new developments in technology, architecture, medicine, health, etc. With the internet developing so quickly in the last decade, every aspect of our lives will be becoming more digital and these STEM majors only help to further that trend.

Though most people think of engineering/technology when they think of STEM, STEM majors also comprise of the majors commonly found in the healthcare industry. Doctors, nurses, veterinarians, lab technicians, and biologists are all examples of healthcare professionals that have a bright future. This is because these fields are not as trendy as others and look to be around for as far ahead as we can predict. Though obviously job/career success is never guaranteed just because one has majored in a specific degree, these STEM majors are as safe as it gets in our rapidly changing economy, where jobs are disappearing left and right.

These majors are a solid choice if financial stability is very important to you and you are passionate about these fields. By looking ahead to the future, we can really begin to see what types of professions will be in demand. In demand jobs usually equal a decent pay scale. Additionally, the more demand there is within a specific field, the more options the employee will have when it comes to financial leverage to negotiate or choose between multiple job opportunities.

You may visit the school or university you have in mind for a fairly accurate estimate of how much a college major will cost you. There is actually no exact cost of how much you'll pay for college unless you're enrolled. Be reminded that there are other expenses like books, board, and incidental fees aside from tuition.

Based on research done by Discover Student Loans for USA Today, nearly half of adults limit their child's choices based on the price. This is one of the factors that affects students regarding where they want to study and what they want to major in.

When it comes to funding your education, it's important that your expenses do not add to your burdens. For instance, let's say that you happened to choose a college major that requires you to relocate. You have to make sure that you can handle all the expenses involved with the relocation process. Relocating can be a burden on a family, as it adds to living expenses. So ask yourself first if you can afford to move for your education.

It may be a challenge to simultaneously keep all these considerations in mind. Similar to listing your interests, you also need to document factors that affect the actual cost of attending college. These include your personal expenses, transportation, textbooks, supplies, room and board, tuition fees, and other elements affecting cost of college education, including fun!

It is also important to factor in the expectation that your yearly study expenses will slightly increase each semester. Otherwise, you will be putting yourself in a financial frenzy or at least setting yourself back even further than you had planned. While students are yet to find a way to determine at what rate tuition fees will increase yearly, reliable estimates from public agencies provide them a vantage point in terms of budget management.

A report from the National Center for Education Statistics (NCES) shows non-profit public colleges' average annual tuition fee is $13.6 thousand. On the other hand, non-profit private colleges' average yearly tuition fee is at $36 thousand. NCES also included in these figures additional expenses students may incur while attending college.

Your study expenses may also fall behind or go above the average, based on your college major. Remember that your major's curriculum dictates the number of subjects or credit hours you will need to complete yearly. Obviously, the more credit hours you need to complete, the higher your tuition fee is. STEM majors usually require more credit hours than other majors.

Another consideration when estimating your study expenses is the college's location. Are you paying an in-state or out-of-state tuition fee? An in-state tuition fee is typically lower. Practically, it is financially wise to enroll in an in-state college - all things being equal. Experts put in-state colleges' tuition fees at fifty percent lower than an out-of-state colleges' tuition fees.

The discounted portion of an in-state tuition fee is, in fact, a state government subsidy extended to state taxpayers like your parents or even yourself. If your state college is offering your preferred major anyway, consider enrolling in that institution to extend your finances.

If you will be studying in an out-of-state college, remember to account for the cost of room and board in your total study expenses. On-campus apartments normally cost $9.5 thousand and $11 thousand dollars in public and private colleges, respectively. These figures do not include your meals yet, the cost of which will vary depending on what and where you eat.

Your annual expenses are also affected by textbooks and supplies cost. Depending on what subjects you will take for a specific school year, the total cost of these study materials vary. Request for a list of books and supplies you will need for the school year as soon as possible. This allows you to set aside part of your budget ahead of time. It also provides you more time to find cheaper, but well-maintained, secondhand textbooks and supplies.

In any case though, overestimate the total cost for books and supplies. For your reference, NCES puts the yearly cost of textbook and extra school supplies between $1,100 and $1,800. Your college's library may also have multiple copies of these required resource materials, so you may want to borrow them instead.

Living on or off campus warrants setting aside a budget for your transportation needs. Similar to expenses for personal hygiene, clothing and other miscellaneous items, you have complete control of your transportation expenses. Whenever possible, walk or take the campus bus to your classes and save money on gas or public transportation.

Needless to say, you will never come up with an exact estimate of what you'll be spending in real life. However, by overestimating a cost rather than underestimating it provides you leeway to workaround a financial situation off the bat. There will be circumstances in which you will be forced to change what you have set aside for spending on something and it is always more than the budgeted amount. Having more than enough saves you from inconvenient and embarrassing situations.

Besides having an estimate of how much a college major is going to cost you, it's also important to determine how you are going to pay for it. Sometimes it is the parents who support their children's college education. For some, it's self-support as they work for their own education. But there are other sources of financial help out there, like college grants for example. Aside from college scholarships, you can also apply for student loans. Thus, students and parents alike will have to be practical in choosing a university.

The smartest way to support your college education is to get a part-time job. You are not just earning income that can cover a part of your study expenses, but you are also exposing yourself to a work environment you are most likely to experience when you graduate and formally join the workforce.

Experts recommend getting a job that will immediately expose you to your preferred future career. However, your lack of experience may pose challenges. The least you can do is to get a job you can commit to and can offer you flexibility. Based on a study conducted by the Families and Work Institute in 2005, small businesses offer more flexibility to their employees than most large corporations. While small businesses often do not provide a wide range of benefits, the fact that you can negotiate your work schedule is enough for a starter to feel privileged.

You can also get a part-time position at a start-up business with only one or two owners and/or employees. These businesses will definitely need a hand in their operations. Since you are not expected to demand a full-time salary or a range of benefits yet, they are more likely to hire you than an experienced employee looking for stability. In addition, you may even get the opportunity to work from home, as many of these businesses rely on virtual offices to keep their overheads low.

Since national corporations may not hire you yet, you can also apply for a paid part-time job in local establishments like town museums, theaters, city libraries, temples, or churches. Most community, religious, and cultural-based institutions highly depend on part-timers and won't mind paying for part-time service rendered.

Other sectors that target hiring part-timers are federal government agencies, educational institutions (like your school), and sales departments of various local businesses.

After carefully choosing the type of business or sector you would want to work with part-time, start reaching out to your friends, relatives, and teachers to let them know you are looking for part-time employment. The bigger your network is, the better quality and more reliable referrals you will get.

Apart from your network, you can directly communicate with your prospective employers. Most employers find it impressive when someone personally approaches them for possible part-time employment. It gives them a positive impression of your character.

Lastly, make your job search as comprehensive as your college major search by visiting job websites and referring to job boards. At times, your school's bulletin board and student support program can help you find a part-time job. Just don't rely too much on your online search. Job sites often limit their postings to full-time jobs, as many companies that use them want to avoid "dabblers".

Another way to finance your college education is to apply for a student loan. Others avoid getting this type of financial support because of their fear of debt. While there is truth in most of the horror stories you have probably heard about student loans, these tragedies often happen because of the borrower's failure to understand how these loans work.

There are only two general types of student loan – federal and private. The government grants the former and private financial institutions offer the latter. Both types have standard loan terms and conditions that are found in the disclosures part of the loan paperwork. Make sure to read and understand everything stated in the disclosures, especially your payment options.

Remember that you need to pay these loans whether you earn your degree or not. Others tend to overlook and forget about this condition midway from the time their loan is granted. As a result, their credit histories are negatively impacted and their privilege to apply for bigger loans as they move on from college is reduced.

There are also loan terminologies that you want to understand before applying for a student loan. Understanding these terms will allow you to strategize how you are going to pay it off.

Loan Deferment

This is a set period when your loan is postponed for any reason, although this is typically voluntary on the part of the borrower.

Capitalized Interest

This is when an unpaid interest is added on your principal, which increases the subsequent amount of interest. For example, your installment due last month is $500 with an interest of 1%. You only paid $450. Your current month's due is computed as follows:

- $500 (Fixed Monthly Installment) + $5 (Unpaid Interest) x 1% = $6.05 (Interest for this Month)

- $500 + $50 (Unpaid Balance from Last Month) + $6.05 = $556.05 (This Month's Total Due)

The additional charge is very minimal. However, just imagine how this will multiply if you frequently fail to pay your monthly dues in full.

Grace Period

This is a period of time after college before the government or the financial institution will require you to repay the loan.

Now that you have an idea about the most common terms you will be dealing with when you apply for a student loan, it is time to understand the types of federal student loans that you can apply for. Remember, you are required to check what the government can offer before you can explore what private financial institutions can provide.

Direct and Subsidized Loan

Depending on what the government determines as your financial needs based on their regulations, you may be granted a certain amount for this loan. This type will not charge you interest for at least 50% of your attendance in college and during deferment.

Direct and Non-Subsidized Loan

Unlike the previous loan, it is your school which determines the loan amount the government should grant to you. The amount is based on the cost of your college attendance, minus any financial aid you receive while attending college. You will be charged interest while in college, during deferment and grace periods. Capitalized interest also applies to this type of loan.

Direct Plus Loan

Also unsubsidized, this type of loan may be granted to your parents or guardians, the amount of which depends on the cost of your college attendance minus all financial aid you receive while studying. It also charges interest in all periods, plus gets capitalized the month following the failed payment of full balance.

For more information on these loans, you may visit the Office of the US Department of Education's Federal Student Aid website at www.fafsa.ed.gov_

On the other hand, you have the private student loan option, which you should only consider as a supplement to a federal student loan previously granted. This means you only apply for this type of loan with the intention of offsetting study expenses not covered by a federal student loan.

Since a private student loan is generally offered by a profit-based financial institution like a bank or a loan company such as Sallie Mae, expect the application process to be as tedious as the process for getting a credit card. Before any financial institution grants you a study loan, they will check your credit score to determine if your application will be approved or rejected based on their specific requirements. If your application is approved, your credit history will still be used to assess the amount of loan you will receive and the monthly interest rate.

The lender also considers your credit score in stipulating the terms and conditions of the loan, and any additional feature like specialized loan repayment terms. This is indeed not the easiest route to receive a student loan, considering that its approval primarily depends on your credit standing. At your age, it is only logical that you do not have a solid credit history yet. So, what is the workaround?

It certainly is questionable why financial institutions will even offer this type of loan when they are most likely to decline applications from students who mostly do not have a credit history yet. However, most financial institutions accept a co-signer to back up an application without a significant credit history. If you are going this route, get a co-signer whose credit score is impressive enough to increase the chances of your loan application getting approved.

Experts recommended checking the websites of these private financial institutions that offer student loans before attempting to inquire in person. Checking their requirements, as well as their terms and conditions beforehand can save you valuable time and effort.

When you shop around, check for loan elements that can impact its overall cost and the convenience of repaying it. For instance, interest rate can either be fixed or variable. Considering how volatile the financial market is, going for a loan with a fixed interest rate is a wiser move than a loan with variable interest. Also, consider the length of the grace period. A longer grace period helps you gain financial momentum, while a short one can possibly mess with how you manage your finances.

Another important factor you should keep your eye on when reviewing student loan products is the repayment plan. For how long will you pay your overdue installments with interest? Is it 12 months, 24 months, 36 months, more? How much will your monthly payment be.

Last but not least, aim for a student loan product that features borrower perks. Some banks will reward you by extending your repayment plan or reducing interest rate if certain requirements are met. These requirements may include regular on-time payments, auto-debit enrollment, and an impressive academic performance.

One key that must be stressed here, is to look at this financial investment of your college education as a long-term investment. This means, there is no reason to go into huge amounts of debt if you can avoid it. Many young people these days go into deep debt in order to get a college degree when most of the time, they could have paid off their degree during their collegiate years, or maybe a few years after graduation.

Don't be afraid to take a few extra years to graduate if it means you can work 15-20 hours a week throughout college and avoid the huge hill of debt you have to climb upon graduation.

This can also affect your decision to go to your preferred university or choosing a major that may be more time-intensive. Engineering degrees are a great example of degrees that often take up to 4-7 years to complete. It is rare that you will see a student enter a college and breeze through an engineering degree in three years.

So based on your preferred degree, make sure to account for if you will have time to work on the side, or if you'll need to commit more hours to school than some of your other classmates who don't have courses that are as time-consuming as yours.

Again, the long-term investment mindset will allow you to plan ahead and realize that whether you graduate in 4 years, 5 1/2 years, or 7+ years, isn't as important as choosing the correct major and working towards completing it at your own pace.

Chapter 3:

Your Marketable Skills and Potential Of Interests

Some people say that following one's passion means sending themselves to the poorhouse. Don't get confused, as this idea is a bit contrary to the first chapter. What you need to know is that passion is not the only thing you must consider in choosing a college major.

Just think of this: pursuing a college major is like pursuing a business: You know what you can sell to people. You know your target market. But does it follow the demand and supply principle? Is there a salary potential with what you do? It just goes to show that passion is not enough. Follow your dream but also have an understanding of where you want to be financially and how to get there.

This is where it becomes important to know the lifestyle you want to live. This doesn't mean you must know what age you want to get married and have kids at, but having some type of general guidelines to the lifestyle you want to live is very important. Some people love to work long hours and get an adrenaline rush from high stress jobs.

The jobs in the New York Stock Exchange are a great example. Stock traders have high stress, long hours, and often unpredictable success rates. Some people thrive in these circumstances, while others prefer a much lower stress, less time-consuming profession such as becoming a teacher. Even the difference in lifestyles is apparent for an elementary school teacher versus a college professor, although they can both be categorized as "teachers".

Also, be honest with yourself if you feel that you want a high paying job to support a more expensive lifestyle. At the end of the day, it is your decision to make when it comes to what type of lifestyle you want to live, but it is obvious that there are people who are content on a $1,000,000/year salary and there are others that are content on a $30,000/year salary. Knowing what types of expenses you want to have can aid in deciding what type of major to choose.

Marty O'Connell, an executive director and the author of "Colleges that Change Lives", said that it's a much more difficult process for students who know what they want, but change their minds, than students who come into college undecided.

There are fields of study that demand you to make decisions as early as possible. For instance, medical schools normally have Pre-Med classes that one needs to plan out well in advance. Says Matt Sanchez, an assistant director of recruiting at the University of Texas in Dallas, students who wish to attend medical school will have to make a decision early on in their collegiate career, in order to have a strong chance.

Keep this in mind if you are thinking of choosing a career that requires a graduate degree or beyond!

Not too long ago, psychologists discovered six major working styles in people. Each working style comprises of one primary and two secondary personality traits. As early as possible, discover how your working style will fit in with your passions.

This is to help you decide on what degree you will need to earn. Understanding your working style years ahead of your competition also lessens the burden of getting the job you want after graduation. In the first place, who wouldn't want to hire someone whose college credentials don't just fit the mold, but also matches the working style needed in the post?

Psychologists named these working styles based on what defines them - realistic, investigative, artistic, social, enterprising, and conventional.

A person with a realistic working style is someone who prefers doing technical work. This person often enjoys outdoor activities or anything related to a sport. Coaches, trainers, athletes, and construction workers are said to possess this style.

Someone with an investigative style loves spending his/her time thinking. When a person is motivated by mental challenges, it is possible that they will have this working style in the future. If you love conducting scientific research, or maybe analyzing and solving problems using scientific methods, you may want to pursue a college degree that will enhance this working style. People who possess this style are mostly inclined to become forensic investigators, laboratory researchers, etc.

An artistic style is commonly found in actors, musicians, artists, etc. Art majors such as Music, Communications, and Fine Arts promote the development of this working style.

A social style is possessed by anyone who is inclined to volunteer for community service.

People with this style often have impeccable interpersonal skills. If you enjoy community work or interactions, this may be your primary style. College majors that can help you enhance this style are Education and Sociology, among others.

Probably the most common among the working styles, the enterprising style is found in leaders, salespeople, and businessmen. Numerous college majors promote this working style, but the most obvious are Business courses. If you see yourself setting up your own business or climbing up the corporate ladder five to ten years from now, choose a major that will hone this style.

A person who excels in organizational and numerical pursuits is said to possess the conventional style. If you always find yourself wanting to solve mathematical equations or finding out ways to increase efficiency, there are various college majors that will enhance your style. These include accountancy, computer science, mathematics, physics, and others.

In conclusion, a reasonable prediction and understanding of your working style well ahead of time allows you to find a college major which considerably matches it. Furthermore, it brings you closer to people who share the same mindset, both at school and at work.

While a comprehensive psychological test is required to determine what your dominant and support working styles are, the overview puts you ahead of the pack. Most importantly, at this point, it leads you to the path of choosing a college major that supports you.

Chapter 4:

Conduct a Bit of Research

It's essential to familiarize yourself with potential college majors that interest you. You may be asking ask, "What for? I'm going to study about it in the next four years anyway". The main reason for this is that you ought to have an idea of what to expect with that field of study. You may take a look at that course's curriculum to see if the subjects truly appeal to you.

Ellain, a freshman student, began college as a Psychology major but switched to Communication Arts. She regrets choosing a course that she really didn't like, as her mother was the one who decided for her to take it. She received good grades in some subjects but she failed in two others.

Since then, she's decided to try another major and this time it is what she really wants to pursue. She's happy with her decision and she's motivated to study. The only downside is that she's starting all over as a first-year student.

However, not all students are given a second chance to start all over again. Monica, now a college senior, majored in Biomedical Engineering. She was complicit with outside influences coming out of high school; but once she got to school, she realized her major was not quite the right one for her. She learned afterwards that she should have picked what was going to make her the happiest.

What happened to Ellain and Monica are just two in thousands of similar scenarios. Many college students shift majors because they find the subjects difficult or simply because they are not happy anymore. Nobody wants to fail miserably and end up dropping out of college. If you don't want to regret this in the future, it's best to conduct a bit of research on the coursework firsthand.

If you see that you must take a heavy load of math classes but you don't enjoy math at all, you may want to see if there are alternative routes you can go. Similarly, you can apply this to reading and writing if you seem to struggle in these courses. A few introductory courses in a subject you dislike is no big deal, but having to take harder courses can affect you later on down the road if you don't do a little research before hand.

Spend some time learning what is really involved in different fields of study. This is important especially if you are planning to apply for scholarships. There are good resources for finding college major lists and descriptions, one example is a college course catalog. It is usually published by schools on their online portals so that it will be easy for prospective students to know and compare the descriptions of various majors.

According to Andy Chan, vice president of career development at Wake Forest University, both students and parents should shower themselves with questions regarding different majors. Schools can help by offering assessment tools. Additionally, career services and departments can help you learn about a specific major before you commit.

According to Carmen Varejcka-McGee, an academic adviser at the University of Nebraska in Lincoln, many students get stuck on the idea that they ought to have a clear vocational goal in order to select a major. Now, can you use social media to choose your major? Technology is a great way to enable peer to peer interaction, minus the pressure of asking from school authorities.

Wayfinder, a site developed by the University of Texas at Austin is an interactive website integrated with social media. There, students can get help in choosing their academic majors. They offer self assessments and videos regarding academic paths and careers. Aside from Wayfinder, you may also use other social media channels like LinkedIn and Google+.

As you probably have heard , there are also college major quizzes online. They consist of questions that will identify which potential majors suit you. Some questions include which type of work environment you prefer and how people view you. You could try My Skills Survey, a questionnaire that will assess your transferable skills. These skills are the abilities you can use as the foundation for a wide range of careers. You could also answer the Careerlink Questionnaire, a five-stage online directory that will suggest majors to you.

Aside from online quizzes, you could also use certain tools like the Map of College Majors. This map is a unique tool that shows the location of popular college majors. Aside from this, you may want to check out Workplace Values Assessment for Job-Seekers. This assessment will help you examine what you value in a potential job, in your career, and your line of work.

A recent report from the US Bureau of Labor Statistics and Payscale highlights fifteen of the most valuable careers in the country today. These were considered based on the agencies' growth projections until the year 2020 and available compensation data. Review these suggested careers, along with the results of your online assessments to create a viable springboard when choosing your academic course:

Biochemical Engineer

Entry Level Pay: $53.8 thousand/year

Intermediate Level Pay: $97.8 thousand/year

Estimated Growth in Demand: 61.7% until 2020

Biochemical engineers are generally responsible for developing chemical consumer and commercial products. They also conduct research and documentation of products that are both produced from organic and laboratory materials.

Biochemist

Entry Level Pay: $41.7 thousand/year

Intermediate Level Pay: $ 84.7 thousand/year

Growth in Demand: 30.8% until 2020

Biochemists study the different principles affecting the physical and chemical composition of living things. These principles include natural processes such as heredity, cell growth, and development.

Computer Scientist

Entry Level Pay: $56.6 thousand/year

Intermediate Level Pay: $97.9 thousand/year

Growth in Demand: 24.6% until 2020

Computer scientists generally create and design new technology. They also study and implement ways to expand and extend existing ones. A large part of their responsibility also involves solving complex computing problems encountered in the fields of science, medicine, business, and government services, among many others.

Software Engineer

Entry Level Pay: $54.9 thousand/year

Intermediate Level Pay: $87.8 thousand/year

Growth in Demand: 24.6% until 2020

These engineers are responsible for developing computer software. During the development stage, they make sure all engineering principles are applied in all the stages of the development. Oftentimes, they customize computer systems for clients.

Environmental Engineer

Entry Level Pay: $51.7 thousand/year

Intermediate Level Pay: $88.6 thousand/year

Growth in Demand: 21.9% until 2020

Environmental engineers are responsible for creating solutions for environmental issues such as waste management, pollution control, and the like. They make use of engineering principles, chemistry, soil science, and biology to help their clients address environmental concerns. Both public and private sectors hire them to maintain, develop, and improve public health, systematic recycling, etc.

These are the top five careers based on the statistics released by Payscale and the labor agency. Also in the top fifteen are:

Civil Engineer

Geologist

Management Information Systems

Petroleum Engineer

Applied Mathematics

Mathematics

Construction Manager

Finance

Physics

Statistician

Is your preferred career among the top fifteen? If not, do not worry. Notice that most of these careers are broad and interrelated. Therefore, a growth in one sector could mean a growth in at least one other related sector.

For all we know, it is going to be a domino effect. More biochemists could mean more pharmacists, medical representatives, healthcare professionals, etc. The growth in the finance sector could also mean an increase in the demand for banking professionals, stock traders, etc.

Chapter 5:

Ask for Help

One under-utilized but effective tool in your arsenal is to ask for help from academic advisors and peers. Talk to your guidance counselor in high school. If you're already in college and still not certain about your major, you may consult your academic advisor. Your college admissions officer, academic department professors, and college career services office personnel are also good resources.

Remember that high schools and colleges have professionals who are paid to help students choose majors, so don't be afraid to ask. Aside from these school authorities, you may also consult some students enrolled in degree programs at schools and majors you're considering.

Talk to people who have acquired the major you're bearing in mind. Ask the upperclassmen. Someone who has earned a degree in your field of interest can answer your specific questions because they have first-hand experience. They may have valuable advice to give you, as they've been through the process of major selection and more importantly, the coursework. They can also provide you information about the curriculum and work load. This way, you'll determine if the work load is something you are interested in committing to or if you should pursue other interests.

You should also consult with professionals whose careers interest you. Subscribe to their blogs, as many people nowadays are blogging about their careers. Better yet, reach out to them and tell them that you have a few key questions. Ask them to name the pros and cons of their job and what their recommendation to you would be. What were the paths they took? People love to talk about themselves and especially their careers if they are even somewhat successful.

If you're not appeased with second-hand experiences, you could try working before you enter college. It won't hurt to spend "time off" if you want to get real-world experience. Apply for an entry-level job or try some internship programs. Sydney, a college sophomore, said that college students need to understand how an industry works. If you want to find your career path, it also helps to volunteer in activities related to your chosen major. Rosanne, a college junior, wanted to become a neurosurgeon so she started by volunteering at an Alzheimer's home. Like Sydney, Rosanne acquired first-hand experience and applied it to her field of study.

Aside from experienced people, you can also get help from career assessment exams. These career assessments are normally given in high school so that students will have an idea of which college majors they will enjoy. If you have never taken a career assessment exam, it would really benefit you to take one before you select your major. You will probably learn some things about yourself that you never realized before.

All of these different methods are at your disposal and have all been proven to help students come to conclusions. Make sure to take advantage of as many of these as you can.

Chapter 6:

Engaging in Self-Reflection

It's time to engage in serious self-refection. You can do it by asking yourself questions about your past, present, and future. As we have covered, there are several factors to consider when selecting a college major. Yet, there are even a few more things you could ask yourself in order to continue the funneling down process. Some of them are as follows:

How do you see yourself in the next five or ten years? If you see yourself working in an office, you may enroll at courses that are administrative-related. If you see yourself engaging socially, you may want to major in subjects like Business, Psychology, Education, or Communications.

What were your best subjects in high school? While you were in high school, what type of extra-curricular activities did you partake in? These questions will help you examine your abilities, natural inclinations, as well as your honed skills.

What makes you curious and excited to learn more? If you like working with children, you may want to major in Special Education or Child Care Management. If you are the type who loves nature and the outdoors, you may take Environmental Science, Natural Resources Conservation, or Forest Sciences Biology. Or if you are inclined to design and style, great options are Fashion Design, Clothing Textile Studies, or Drafting Design Technology.

To funnel down within a department, start by picking major categories like Arts and Humanities, Business, and Social Sciences. Then have a list of possible majors you could take from those categories. Write down the broad college majors and then break them down from there. If you are interested in getting a Business degree, look at all the options like Accounting, Global Business, Marketing, and others that are more descriptive and specialized.

If you worked in the past, what did you learn about your likes and dislikes with that work experience? List what you loved and didn't love about that previous job. Trying to learn what you love and don't love is a growing experience.

After you've clicked through major profiles on school websites, it's best to ask questions while you read. What do you value in work? Will you enjoy the daily activities in that major? What type of activities does your major emphasize? Most importantly, are you enthusiastic to work hard for the knowledge you'll be offered.

After going through all of these topics, hopefully you have found some guidance to make a solid decision for your future. It is important to remember that you may not know your college major by tomorrow morning, but you need to engage in the exercises and actions listed throughout the book in order to gain some type of traction. The options are all there for you, all you need to do is take advantage of them!

Finally, remember that it is super important to follow your own passion(s) over any other influence in your life. Choosing a college major is a decision that you are going to have to live with and 20 years from now, nobody will care what your parents or friends wanted for you if you aren't happy.

Be courageous through the process and trust in the research that you have put in. You will be able to live with a bad decision, as long as you were the one who made that decision. It is another story to be forced to live with making a bad decision that you didn't want to make in the first place. Good luck in your journey!

41249265R00046

Made in the USA
Middletown, DE
07 March 2017